SPAIN
LAND OF MANY DREAMS

CLB 1529
© 1987 Colour Library Books Ltd., Guildford, Surrey, England
All rights reserved
Printed and bound in Barcelona, Spain by Cronion, S.A.
Published in 1987 by Crescent Books, distributed by Crown Publishers, Inc.
ISBN 0 517 62368 4
h g f e d c b a

SPAIN
LAND OF MANY DREAMS

CRESCENT BOOKS
NEW YORK

Most people come to Spain for its climate and landscape, which is to say that they come for a part of the climate and a part of the landscape, for Spain is nothing if not a land of variety. Sheltered by the inland mountains, eastern Spain receives little rain from the prevailing westerlies and is occasionally swept by hot, dry winds from the Sahara. Edging the seaward side of eastern Spain, from Barcelona to Algeciras, are a succession of wide bays and sandy beaches, and it is this combination of sand, sun and heat which attracts so many of Spain's visitors.

But those three vital commodities are only a tiny part of Spain, and were far from the minds of the first recorded foreigners to visit the country's Mediterranean coast. If anything, the sand may have put them off, while the sun and heat were but pale imitations of those to be found at home. The Phoenicians were drawn to Spain from their home in present day Lebanon by tales of the mineral wealth of Tartessus. Tin from Cornwall, in England, and copper from Spain were mixed at Tartessus, probably near present-day Jerez, to make bronze. The Phoenicians were the great merchants of the ancient world and came in search of the bronze in exchange for goods of their own from the east. More than a thousand years before Christ, a civilisation native to Spain was being influenced by another culture from another country. It was a story that would be repeated throughout Spain's long history. Yet, through all these vicissitudes, the underlying Spanish culture was never lost.

The Phoenicians never attempted a full scale settlement in Spain, coming instead to trade and to make money. Some of their trading stations are still important to Spain, for the Phoenicians had an almost uncanny eye for a good harbour. Cadiz, probably the oldest city in Spain, began as a Phoenician station and takes its name from Gadir, Phoenician for 'fortress'. Malaga, Adra and Villaricos also date back to the time of these traders from the east. When Phoenicia itself fell to Assyria, the colonies in Spain were taken over by Carthage, a Phoenician city in Africa. When Carthage lost a long and

devastating series of wars with Rome, at the close of the third century before Christ, Spain passed to Rome.

With the Romans came the first great reshaping of Spain. This Romanisation was perhaps the most complete of any province in the great empire of the Caesars. In 74 A.D. the entire population of Spain was granted Roman citizenship, an honour not extended to the rest of the Empire for another 140 years. This political advance reflected the massive urbanisation which had taken place in Spain, and the change in outlook of the Spaniards. Nearly all the native languages of the peninsula had been replaced by Latin. Only in the northeast did Latin fail, as have all other languages, to replace Basque. By 98 A.D. the Romanisation of Spain was such that a Spaniard by the name of Marcus Ulpius Traianus was able to assume the purple and become known to history as the Roman Emperor Trajan.

Roman remains lie scattered throughout Spain and form an impressive display. At Alcantara stands one of the most famous Roman sights in the country – an imposing bridge spaning the Tagus in a series of six granite arches. The tallest of the arches towers 150 feet in the air and the granite blocks stay together without the aid of mortar. Though of Roman workmanship, the bridge has been damaged and repaired many times in its long history. The gate-tower, for instance, takes the form of a triumphal arch dedicated to Trajan, but also carries the Royal Arms of the Hapsburgs.

It is at Merida, however, that the finest concentration of Roman remains in Spain is to be found. The town was founded as a colony for retired legionaries, and the civic buildings of the era reflect its importance. The bridge across the Guadiana dates from before Christ and stretches some 2,650 feet on 60 arches. Not to be outdone in splendour, the amphitheatre is an ellipse about 420 feet long with banks of seating and a central arena which hosted gladiatorial and wild-animal fights. It is the theatre, however, which is the true jewel of

Merida. Thirty-two delicate, Corinthian columns stand two storeys high along the facade, while the terraced auditorium could seat 6,000 people. From the highest of these seats a beautiful view of the surrounding ruins can be gained, giving an idea of the splendours of Roman Spain.

One of the most popular modern festivities of Spain brings to mind the ways of the Romans. There are still huge stadiums being maintained in Spainish cities, and numerous small arenas in the villages, for the most exciting of bloodsports.

The origins of bullfighting date back millennia, though it can hardly be dated precisely. In 228 BC a Carthaginian army was advancing on Ilici when it was met by the natives. The Spaniards drove forward a herd of savage bulls which so disrupted the Carthaginian army that it was almost wiped out. When the Romans arrived some years later, they found games in southern Spain in which men artfully dodged a charging bull before killing it with an axe or spear. During the centuries of Roman rule and the Visigothic era which followed, this simple sport developed into the two main branches of the art to be seen today.

In the west the main object of the games is to display the dexterity and skill of the men. The bull's horns are tipped with balls or are padded, while the men indulge in certain tricks, including pole-vaulting over the charging bull, to show their prowess. It is the other form of bullfighting, that practised in most of Spain, in which the bull is killed, which is the more popular and well known. Elaborate ritual has grown up around the bullfight over the centuries, and the death of every bull is surrounded by custom and spectacle.

First, the participants enter in a grand procession, resplendent in their gaily-coloured uniforms. After the rousing welcome given to the men, the bull is released and is first goaded with the cape so that the matador can judge how it is likely to react to his attack. Next, the picadors arrive on horseback to lance the shoulder muscles of the bull. After further play by the matadors, the banderilleros enter the arena with two-foot-long staves decorated with coloured paper. Usually performing on foot, the banderilleros have the difficult task of planting their staves in the shoulders of the bull while avoiding the sharp horns. When several pairs of staves have been skilfully embedded in the great shoulder muscles, thus weakening them and lowering the head, the matador returns.

Now begins the best-known part of the fight. Using his cape, the matador tries to elude the repeated charges of the bull, while remaining as close to the horns as possible and striking an elegant pose. When the bull is sufficiently tired, and the staves in the neck have lowered its head, the 'Hour of Truth' arrives. Drawing his sword, and taking position carefully, the matador runs at the bull and plunges his sword in between the shoulder blades. If done properly this thrust will sever the aorta, the largest artery in the body, and result in almost instant death, though another man is on hand in case the thrust is bungled. The bull's carcass is then butchered outside the ring and either distributed to the poor or sold to the crowd. Though the contest is weighted in favour of the matador, the fight is not totally one-sided. Most matadors expect to suffer some sort of injury at least once a year, and of the 115 accepted master matadors who have dominated the sport in the past three centuries 40 have died in the ring.

If bullfighting originated in ancient times, so did another great tradition of the Spanish: wine-making. Early Greek and Phoenician merchants brought wine to Spain in their amphorae and may even have produced some locally, but it was the Romans who really started wine production. Wine had originated in Mesopotamia in about 6,000 BC and reached Italy about five millennia later. With a thoroughness typical of their Empire, the Romans explored every avenue of viticulture and produced wine which was not to be equalled until an unknown genius discovered what a cork could do, some 300 years ago.

The Romans had just about everything needed to make excellent wine, though whether they actually did so or not is an unanswerable question. They grew vines with great care, and numerous books were written concerning the growing of grapes which would still be valuable today. One writer stated that 'vines love an open hill', a truism emphasised by the fact that the best wines of Spain still come from open hills. Once the grapes had been picked they were carefully fermented before being stored in barrels and bottles, both far better than the porous amphorae used by the Greeks. It was in these barrels and bottles that the benefits of ageing first came to light, and the Romans were eager to take advantage of them. Only good quality, strong wines benefit from age, and the fact that the Romans praised old wines suggests that they were producing just this sort. As with most of the sensual pleasures, the Romans could take ageing wine to excess. The almost legendary vintage of Opimius, produced in 121 BC, was still being drunk and praised several years after the birth of Christ, at an age when, today, even Port might be considered suspect.

With the collapse of the Roman Empire hordes of barbarians – Vandals and Goths – flooded into Spain. But, plunder and destroy as they did, the barbarians fell under the spell of Spanish wine. By the 6th century the Visigoths had set up an independent, Christian kingdom which covered most of Spain. On the whole, the Visigoths were content to remain a privileged ruling class while the Hispano-Romans continued to work the land. With no educated elite at the helm, Roman culture began to fall apart, but wine-making continued under the hot, Spanish sun. Quality may have suffered as tricks of the trade were forgotten and specialised equipment broke, never to be replaced, but production hardly slackened and is today as high as ever. In northwestern Spain vines are still trained among trees as they were in Roman times, and much of the country can trace an unbroken tradition of winemaking back to the Caesars.

Along the upper valley of the Ebro spread the vineyards of Rioja, which produce probably the best red wine in Spain. Francophiles ascribe this to a small and temporary influx of French growers last century, but it is more than likely that Spanish winemakers on the banks of the Ebro just happened to get it right. Be that as it may, the soft, tawny wines of Rioja are produced by bodegas which buy in grapes from the region's multitude of small-scale growers. Once fermented, the wine is stored in great oak barrels for far longer than is usual in other countries, giving it a faint but distinctive vanilla flavour.

It is far to the southwest, near the mouth of the Gaudalquiver River, however, that Spain's truly great wine is to be found. On the chalk hills around Jerez de la Frontera are grown the grapes for the wine to which the town has given its name: sherry. Shipping sherry to all parts of the globe, Jerez depends on the long, time-consuming process of sherry production for its very existence. Once the wine has been produced in the low, whitewashed buildings in the hills, it is brought down to the town for transformation in the solera system. Each bodega has rank upon rank of barrels, which form an integral part of the solera. A certain amount of wine is poured into the first barrel in the rank and mixed with that already in the barrel from previous years. The same amount of mixed wine is then drawn off and poured into the next barrel. The process continues down the long line, with each barrel containing more mature and better mixed wine than the one before. Wine drawn from the final barrel may contain wine decades old and will hardly vary in quality from year to year.

The end result of all this effort and time is not just shipped abroad – much of it is consumed in Jerez itself. Here the sherry is served in little bars by the half bottle, chilled on ice. Accompanied by morsels of savoury food, an iced half-bottle is about the right amount with which to while away a couple of hours in the dazzling heat of southern Spain. Sherry is drunk in many ways in many parts of the world, but perhaps the natives of Jerez have found the best.

Jerez itself is steeped in history. It was near here that the smelters of Tartessus produced bronze so many centuries ago, and just to the south of the town, the Visigothic King Roderick met the Muslim Tariq from North Africa in battle in 711. The Christian Visigoths were slaughtered by the thousand and Tariq found himself in a strange position. Stretching away to the north of the blood-soaked battlefield was a large, rich country whose government and ruling class were nearly all lying dead at his feet. Pausing only for the arrival of a fresh Arab army under Musa, Tariq seized as much of the peninsula as he could for his master the Umayyad Caliph at Damascus. The mass of the peasants bowed to the will of their new rulers, for a Muslim landlord was little different from a Christian one when it came to paying taxes. Only seemingly unimportant Christian fugitives in the northern mountains of Asturia remained free from Muslim domination.

In 722 Pelayo, one of these Visigoth noblemen hiding in the mountains, gathered a force at Covadonga in the depths of the mountains and defeated an equally small force of Muslims. Though Pelayo probably saw this as just another event in a precarious life on the run, later generations looked on Covadonga with the benefit of hindsight. To them, it guaranteed the future independence of a Christian kingdom in the north and marked the beginning of the great Reconquista.

Looming large in both the history and thoughts of Spain, the Reconquista was one of the most dramatic movements in European history. At first it was simply a struggle for survival by such men as Pelayo, but as the Christian states became established and began to grow, the struggle took on a new meaning. It became part of a vision of a unified Spain.

The Christian rulers of the north looked back to the days of Visigothic rule, when the whole peninsula formed one unified Christian kingdom. Religion mixed with nationalism and ambition to create a heady mixture which drove the Christians onwards. For centuries the desire to throw the Muslims out of Spain was the goal of the Christian kings and knights, and a religious crusading spirit long remained part of the Spanish way of life.

In their sumptuous palaces the more educated Arabs may have found such burning ambition in the northern barbarians a little difficult to grasp, particularly as it was far from straightforward. Not only did the Christians war against the Muslims, they also squabbled interminably amongst themselves. It was as well for the Christian states that the Muslims were adept at exactly the same type of internecine struggle. For the men of the time, of course, religious and nationalistic ideals were all very well as ideals, but personal safety, wealth and power were of more immediate concern.

Perhaps the greatest hero of the Reconquista is known as El Cid, and his career reveals the ideals and contradictions of the movement. Rodrigo Diaz de Vivar was born in 1043 into the minor nobility of the Christian kingdom of Castile. As soon as he attained manhood, El Cid plunged into the turmoil of the Reconquista with energy, and by the age of 22 was the leader of the royal troops of Castile. Having severely defeated the Muslims in a series of battles, Diaz loyally followed his master, King Sancho, into a particularly bitter internecine struggle with his royal brother. In 1072 Sancho was killed and the brother, Alfonso VI, an enemy of El Cid, came to the throne. El Cid promptly lost his position and honours, though he remained at the Castilian court. In 1081 El Cid led a private raid on the Muslim kingdom of Toledo, but the Muslim ruler was a friend of Alfonso and El Cid was banished.

Thereafter, El Cid's fortunes changed. With no country to call home and no money to his name, he had to live as best he could. The only trade he knew was fighting; after all he had never been beaten in battle, and he sold his sword to the Muslim ruler of Saragossa. For some years El Cid was embroiled in the warfare between the Muslim kingdoms and at one time he even soundly defeated a Christian army. The great hero of the Reconquista seems to have been more concerned with himself at this stage, and so he was to remain for the rest of his life. After a brief return to Castile in 1087, El Cid embarked on his greatest private venture. Using deft political manoeuvres as much as his fighting abilities, El Cid emerged as the ruler of the rich kingdom of Valencia. Though nominally acting for Castile, El Cid ruled independently and in great splendour at Valencia for the last five years of his life. He tolerated his subjects' Muslim faith and made little attempt to extend Christianity or to reunite Spain. After his death, however, Valencia passed to Castile, and the undoubted valour and skill of El Cid on the battlefield became an example for many of the Christian knights who followed him.

The Reconquista rumbled on for centuries after the death of El Cid. When the area around Jerez fell to the Christians in 1262, however, it was all but over. Only the unimportant, but prosperous, Muslim state of Granada remained, and that finally disappeared in 1492.

The long centuries of warfare, division and bitterness left their marks on the land, marks that can still be found today. Not that there are many Muslims left in the areas which were once controlled by them. Such institutions as the Inquisition, and instructions either to leave or to turn to Christ, were common after the fall of Granada and within a short time the entire peninsula was uncompromisingly Catholic. Yet differences remain and regionality is a key component of Spain. Areas longest under Muslim control have numerous monuments to the defeated culture, and the variety of languages which come under the blanket heading of Spanish is bewildering. Of course, the dream of a united peninsula was never brought about, and Portugal remains an independent country, while the Basques had never been integrated with Roman or Visigothic Spain and remain culturally distinct to this day.

Granada, the last bastion of the Muslims to fall, has an atmosphere at once typically Spanish and totally unique. The sheer beauty of the setting and the majesty of the architecture have turned the entire city into a national monument. Overlooking the town from its hilltop is the Alhambra, the mediaeval palace of the Muslim kings and one of the wonders of Spain. It has been argued that the magnificent decoration to be found within the plain exterior of this building is the finest of any Arabian palace. The interwoven complex of towers, rooms and courtyards is festooned with intricate carvings of a quality and quantity not found elsewhere. In the Court of the Lions, for instance, a fountain of 12 black marble lions spout water surrounded by more than a hundred beautifully carved columns. It is perhaps the sheer delicacy of the stonework and decoration which makes the Alhambra so charming and irresistible. Life amongst its arcades and halls must have been almost idyllic for the rulers of Granada when they were at the height of their power.

The Christian takeover produced a rash of building as the new masters proclaimed their power and faith in stone. The most prestigious building they erected was a testament to the religion in the name of which they had conquered the Muslims. The Cathedral was begun just thirty years after the Christian conquest, but was not completed until 1703. Though begun in the Gothic style, the cathedral eventually emerged as the most splendid Renaissance church in Spain, with a mighty interior and spectacular facade.

Not only is the cathedral a masterpiece of architecture, it contains a wealth of art treasures. Statues, paintings and tapestries crowd the interior, which is topped by the 158-foot-high dome of the Capilla Mayor.

South, beyond the mountains of the Sierra Nevada, can be found examples of the architecture of a more modern period, displaying the wealth the region has found in recent years. From Sotogrande to Almeria run 250 miles of towns and villages better known under their collective name of the Costa del Sol. The resorts of the Costa del Sol generally attract brash holiday publicity, but less than favourable comments from those who consider themselves to have good taste. Yet the very popularity of the region indicates that the resorts must have something, and their prominence is a great accomplishment for the Spanish.

A few decades ago the entire stretch of coastline was empty of both hotels and foreigners. There were many quiet fishing villages, together with the occasional larger port. Luxurious vegetation backed the long, sandy beaches and whitewashed houses clustered together in cheerful communities in an almost idyllic climate. The whole area was perfect as a holiday resort, except for one thing: it was difficult to reach. Most of the people who had enough spare time and money to indulge in holidays lived far to the north and had enough trouble reaching the south of France, never mind the south of Spain. Cut off by the high sierras and their primitive roads, the land route was long and arduous, enough to ruin any holiday before it began, and the sea route was almost as bad.

It was the large passenger aircraft which made the Costa del Sol. Flying into Malaga Airport in search of the sun, the people of northern Europe then fanned out along the coast. The sudden influx of visitors brought not only wealth, but a problem: more people wanted to come than could be accommodated. For once the Spaniards had to abandon their somewhat relaxed attitude to time, and they did it with a will. Within an incredibly short period

modern hotels, the envy of most of Europe, sprang up along the coast, and a whole array of facilities was built to cater for the visitor. Today, the Costa del Sol is one of the few areas of Europe totally geared to holidays. So complete is the transformation that visitors need not stir more than a few steps from their hotels to find almost any kind of fun they may desire.

Further to the northeast lies the great maritime town of Cartagena. Though there is not much here to interest the passing tourist, Cartagena is one of the oldest and most prestigious cities in Spain. Aptly enough for a naval base, the city was founded by the Carthaginians in 221 BC, when they were the most powerful maritime power in the Mediterranean. The city name derives from its ancient title of Carthago Nova, New Carthage. In fact, the actual founder was Hasdrubal Barca, father of the more famous Hannibal who led a Spanish army, including elephants, across the Alps to attack Rome. Over the years the magnificent natural harbour at Cartagena has been the key to the city's fortunes and even today Cartagena exports the produce of the local area: olive oil, minerals and dried fruit.

While Cartagena marks the southern end of the Costa Blanca, yet another stretch of idyllic, sandy coastline, Valencia marks its northern end. As in the days when El Cid carved a holding for himself, Valencia is one of the most important cities in Spain. Three-quarters of a million people live in the city, making it the third largest in the nation. Yet, despite its great growth, the city has never lost its vibrant, southern atmosphere. Under the generally cloudless skies which dominate this part of Spain, it is the old city which remains the most important and colourful area of the metropolis. All year long the narrow streets echo to the shouts of passers-by and shopkeepers as they bustle along beneath shuttered and balconied windows. In March the city really comes alive as Fallas, a festival in honour of San Jose, takes place. Huge papier-maché figures, destined to be burnt at midnight on the last day of the festival, are set up in the street, towering high above the heads of the citizens.

Valencia makes much of its living from its position as provincial capital and from industry, but it gained its early importance from La Huerta, the fertile plain which surrounds the city. It was during the years when the Arabs ruled Valencia that the two crops for which the region is so famous were first cultivated. The rivers running down from the hills were tamed and used to irrigate the land so that oranges and rice could be grown. Once rice was being grown in quantity the Valencians were able to create their most famous product: paella. Many people throughout the world have had good reason to thank the Valencians for that invention. The coloured rice, bedecked with mussels, clams, prawns and other seafood, is one of the most appetising dishes in Spain. Though other towns have taken paella and adapted it to their local resources, it is that of Valencia which remains the favourite.

Another delicious fish dish is to be found in the great city of Barcelona, to the north. Zarzuela is a dish of fish, lobster, shellfish and almonds stewed in white wine, and is as inextricably linked with Catalonia as the language which predominates here. Quite different from the Castilian language, which foreigners think of as Spanish, Catalonian developed behind the mountain barriers which cut the area off from the rest of Spain. The whole attitude of the Catalonians has long been dominated by the thought that they are different from the other Spaniards and should be treated as such.

In part this difference in culture and language may be explained by the long historical barrier between Catalonia and the rest of Spain. The Moors only held the region for eighty years after the collapse of the Visigothic kingdom before they were overthrown by the Franks from the north. Catalonia played little part in the long struggle with the Muslims, and only joined Spain in the 12th century as the result of a dynastic marriage. In centuries past Catalonia enjoyed a great measure of freedom from the central government, but this disappeared in the wake of the Civil War in the 1930s. Nonetheless, Catalonia retains its individuality and is, in many ways, the most European part of Spain.

Barcelona, said to take its name from the Carthaginian Barca family which founded both it and Cartagena, has none of the southern atmosphere of Valencia. Like most of Catalonia, it is more concerned with business. The two million people who live in and around the city manage to turn out about a fifth of the industrial output of the nation. Financial institutions, such as banks and insurance companies, also have their home in the city. All the industries, which include car and heavy machinery manufacture, textiles and chemicals, depend on the large port facilities for transport. Yet Barcelona has no natural harbour, such as can be found at Cartagena and Valencia, and in 1400 there was nothing more than an open roadstead. The first mole was constructed in 1474, and development has continued ever since. Today, the harbour covers 700 acres and can boast seven miles of docks. Standing on the harbour

front is a massive iron column topped by a bronze statue of Christopher Columbus. As a further tribute to the man who discovered America, a replica of his ship, the Santa Maria, lies in the harbour itself.

From the Columbus Monument a wide, tree-lined avenue, known as the Ramblas, runs through the heart of the old city towards the great Plaza de Cataluna. The long, shady walk of the Ramblas is always a colourful sight, packed as it is with street traders. On either side of the Ramblas stretches the mediaeval town, with its dark, narrow streets and fine mediaeval cathedral.

To the north of the city work continues on a church which was begun in 1882. The plans of this grand church call for a total length of 350 feet, 12 towers of equal height and a truly magnificent dome some 520 feet tall. Unfortunately, all that has been completed in over a century is the eastern facade, the crypt and the apse, although it is confidently expected that the church will be finished one day.

The unhurried way in which the Spaniards build their churches is perhaps indicative of their whole attitude to time. Impatience is almost unknown in Spain and few people are ever late, for very little ever starts on time. This is particularly true of meals. More than one unprepared visitor has felt the pangs of hunger begin to gnaw as the hands of the clock creep round past not only his normal dinner time, but perhaps his normal bedtime as well.

Eventually, the Spanish hosts get round to eating and drinking while the small hours crawl round the clock. The Spaniards' apparent immunity to late hours might be something of a puzzle, but it can easily be explained. Unlike the cold northern countries, where every scrap of winter sunlight must be utilised, Spain has far too much sunshine. During the blistering heat which scorches the country at noon in the summer it is impossible to work, or even to think coherently, so the Spaniards do not bother to try. Instead, they take to the cool interiors of their houses or shady refuges and put their feet up for a siesta while flies and foreigners buzz around in the heat.

One of the great churches of Spain which benefited from this lack of concern for time is the Cathedral of Nuestra Senora del Pilar in Saragossa. The church has its origins in AD 40, when St James the Great, one of Christ's closest followers, came to Spain and, on the banks of the Ebro, had a vision of the Virgin Mary. A pillar was erected to mark the spot and around this have been built a succession of churches. The present cathedral was begun in 1515 but work continued predictably slowly until 1677. In that year Francisco de Herrera, whose father built El Escorial near Madrid, was put in charge and extensive work in the Baroque style was carried out. The effort could not be sustained, however, and in 1753 a fresh spurt of building under Ventura Rodriquez added many Classical touches to the church. The interior of the main dome was finally painted in the 19th century and the church was complete. The end result is a building of great beauty and splendour whose silhouette is striking in the extreme, with its mass of towers, cupolas and central dome. At the heart of this great monument can still be found the humble pillar where St James received his vision.

Saragossa was the capital of Aragon until the unification of Spain in 1479, when the court moved to Castile. But Saragossa has never forgotten its role as capital of the bare, upland country of Aragon and has retained many traditions quite different from those of the rest of Spain. The city houses a large and important university and is home to an archbishop, underlining its past importance. The Aragonese have their own national costume of slashed, black velvet jacket, knee breeches with a red waist sash, and hemp sandals. The Aragonese have likewise kept up a love of freedom and an intense sense of pride, both of which were outraged in the spring of 1808.

In that year Napoleon Bonaparte, Emperor of France, kidnapped the King of Spain and forced him to abdicate the throne in favour of Napoleon's own brother, Joseph. The horrified citizens of Saragossa rose in revolt against their new, foreign king. Napoleon descended upon the city with the might of the French army, surrounding the city and bombarding it with his cannon. Throughout the rest of 1808 and well into the following year the citizens of Saragossa held out against the power of France. When they were finally forced to surrender, half the inhabitants of Saragossa were dead and their proud city was a ruin. But Saragossa had won a victory far greater than Napoleon's. During the long months of the siege the message of revolt had swept through Spain and a sizeable British army, under the command of the future Duke of Wellington, had arrived to help. France was faced with a war which was to last until Napoleon fell and Spain was free once more. In 1838 the city featured in another struggle between rival claimants to the throne and gained the title it still proudly boasts: 'the always heroic and immortal'.

Northwest of Aragon, around the upper valley of the Ebro, stretches the ancient kingdom of Navarre. Although the area around Pamplona fell under Muslim rule in 711 with the rest of Spain, the Basques maintained their language and culture as they had done under both the Romans and the Visigoths. Within a lifetime the Basque landlords had managed to ignore enough Muslim edicts and wheedle enough local privileges for one Inigo Arista to proclaim himself independent. By 860 the Basques were calling their land an independent kingdom and nobody was strong enough to gainsay them.

Throughout the Middle Ages the kingdom of Navarre held an important and respected position in European politics. However, unlike the rest of the Spanish kingdoms, Navarre did not play a large part in the Reconquista. Once they had freed the Basques and united them, the Kings of Navarre were content to build up their wealth and to control the most accessible passes into France. In Navarre, the Basques were able to continue their ancient customs and way of life while at the same time tolerating those of the Moor and Frank minorities which lived in the land.

The Basques are perhaps the most enigmatic people in Spain. Of all the groups – Castilians, Catalonians and Aragonese for example – the Basques have evidently been in Spain the longest, yet their recorded history is no longer than any other. The language of the Basques, known to themselves as Euskara, is quite clearly not one of the vast Indo-European family of languages. This marks it out from almost every other language of Europe. The language, and, by implication, the people who speak it, is clearly a leftover from the days of Tartessus. When the waves of Indo-Europeans – who include all the speakers of Germanic, Latin, Celtic, Slavonic and Greek languages – poured across Europe from the east, only the Basques managed to hold out. At least that is the conjecture. Basque is certainly non-Indo-European and seems to predate the arrival of the Celts and Greeks, but the Basques do not enter the written record until almost the creation of the Kingdom of Navarre in the 9th century. Before that time there is only an occasional reference to a tribe known as the Vascones, who may or may not have been Basques.

That apart, the culture of the Basques picks them out as clearly as their language. They have always been known as smallholders who have a strong sense of family loyalty and an ability to make a living from a small patch of earth and some sheep. At the same time, Basque seafarers were in the forefront of the exploitation of the fishing grounds off the eastern coast of Canada at the close of the 15th century and they sailed on the first circumnavigation of the globe.

At the same time as Basque fishermen and whalers were reaching the zenith of their power and prosperity, the Basque homeland was losing its political power. By 1232 the native Basque royal family of Navarre had died out and French relatives came to the throne. French influence became dominant in the court and government as the essential Basque culture grew divorced from the Kingdom of Navarre. In 1512 King Ferdinand II of Aragon seized the lands of Navarre which lay south of the Pyrenees, and the King of Navarre, resident in his lands north of the mountains, was powerless to stop him. Navarre continued as an independent kingdom north of the Pyrenees for another 70 years when, due to dynastic machinations, King Henry of Navarre became Henry IV of France. For the past four centuries the Basques have been divided between France and Spain, a situation which most of them have accepted whilst remaining unconvinced of its merits.

The ancient capital of Navarre was Pamplona, and it is still the chief city of the province and remains the seat of an archbishop. The city, however, is best known for its great fiesta. For a fortnight in July this flourishing agricultural centre turns itself over to festivities and merrymaking. Parades of 'giants' and 'bigheads' march through the streets and bullfights take place daily. The most important feature of the Sanfermines, named for Saint Fermin in whose honour the festival is held, takes place every morning amid much excitement and not a little danger. The heart of the city is a maze of narrow, mediaeval streets at the centre of which lies the bull ring. Every morning at seven o'clock the bulls which have been selected for that day's fighting are let loose in the streets of the city. The young men of the city, eager to display their courage to each other and the senoritas, run through the streets. Trying to dodge clear of the bulls' horns while at the same time keeping as close to the bulls as possible, the young men run with red scarves tied around their necks in imitation of bullfighters' capes. In their eagerness to prove their bravery many take risks, and injuries, even deaths, are not uncommon.

It is through Pamplona that the famous Camiño de Santiago makes its way to the west. Usually rendered in English as the 'Way of St James', this ancient route for centuries carried pilgrims from beyond the Pyrenees to the magnificent cathedral at Santiago de Compostella. The same traditions which placed St James the Great's

vision of the Virgin Mary at Saragossa continue to trace a career for St James only partly borne out by the Bible. Having visited the valley of the Ebro, St James returned to the Holy Land and was beheaded by King Herod Agrippa I. After his martyrdom, St James' earthly remains were carried back to Spain to be deposited at Santigo de Compostella, where they now lie in the cathedral crypt.

On their long journey from the Pass of Roncesvalles to the tomb of the saint, the medieval pilgrims passed along a recognised route which was furnished with all the conveniences of more modern highways. At Roncesvalles they could gaze upon the battlefield where the heroic Roland lost his life to vengeful Basques not, as later poets would have it, treacherous Moors. Once down from the high mountains, monasteries and other religious houses lined the route, offering food and a shelter safe from marauding bandits. Hostels were erected and run by local bishops and secular authorities to help the pilgrims in their long walk and, incidentally, to make some money out of them.

West of Pamplona, then the flourishing capital of Navarre, the pilgrims would have completely bypassed and ignored a small town which has since become the most important town in the Basque Provinces. Bilbao is not, however, particularly Basque in outlook. Amid the industrial landscape and urban society of this great city, with its massive population, Basque traditions, language and culture have languished. Always wedded to its home amongst the smallholders of a rural economy, the Basque way of life has never succeeded in establishing a foothold in cities of any size.

In one way, however, the town bears the mark of its Basque ancestry, for it was from seafaring that it gained its first prosperity. Throughout the Middle Ages and after the unification of Spain the citizens of Bilbao made their quiet living by exporting the iron ore and agricultural produce of the surrounding land. But after the sacking of the town by Napoleon's troops, and continual sieges during the Carlist Wars, the citizens decided to rebuild their town. They did it so well that in the past century a massive drive to industrialisation and shipping has fostered a population of nearly half a million.

The town through which the pilgrims did in fact pass had far more to recommend itself five centuries ago than did Bilbao. Some would argue that it still does. Logrono is a small and ancient town on the banks of the Ebro and at the heart of the Rioja. It is, therefore, of prime importance to the Spanish wine industry. The town is also endowed with a fine collection of churches, while six miles to the southwest stands an old equestrian statue of St James.

West of Logrono the Way of St James moves away from the Ebro and climbs over the northern shoulder of the Sierra de la Demanda to drop down into the valley of the Arlanzon. Overlooking this river from a castle-crowned hill is the city of Burgos, long famous for its cathedral, which was as popular with mediaeval pilgrims as it is with modern tourists. The great Gothic edifice, in many ways the finest in Spain, was constructed of a peculiar white limestone of great beauty and still dominates the whole city. It was begun in 1221 and, unusually for a Spanish cathedral, completed in about a century. The open-work spires were, more characteristically, not added until 1442.

Master Enrique, the builder called upon to plan Burgos Cathedral, had already displayed his talent in another great church on the Way of St James. Sixteen years earlier Bishop Manrique of Lara had commanded that a new cathedral be built at Leon, and Master Enrique had the job of designing it. The workers of Leon, however, do not seem to have been as enthusiastic as those of Burgos and the walls had barely risen above their foundations when Master Enrique left for his new job to the east. Imposing as the facade of the cathedral is, the interior is far superior. This is not unusual in Spanish churches, but it is the light which makes Leon so unique. Nowhere else does the sunlight glint through the stained glass quite as it does here, bathing the flagstone floor with a kaleidoscope of shifting colours.

Outside the beautiful cathedral and grand city, Leon seems something of an anticlimax. Poor soils and an unfavourable climate shape the landscape. The little pastureland which survives is given over to the raising of sheep and fighting bulls, while cork oaks grow wherever they can. The cork oak is of vital importance to Spain's wine industry, and that of other countries, and Spain produces an abundance of the material. As their name suggests, these trees provide the cork which seals the necks of bottles. But the trees need careful attention if they are to give good cork. The rough outer bark must be stripped off, while leaving the inner bark undamaged. In an effort to repair the damage done, the tree produces the spongy wood as a sheath around the inner bark. When this has reached a sufficient thickness it is stripped off and the process begins again.

The importance of the cork is that it allows wine to be kept. Prior to 1700 wine was stored and transported in barrels, flasks and a host of other receptacles. But none of these was satisfactory, for they were either not airtight or they imparted an unpleasant flavour to the wine over a period of time. The glass bottle sealed by cork enabled wine merchants to keep their wine for long periods of time in containers which were both airtight and did not affect the taste of the wine. In these bottles wine is able to mature and reach its finest state.

Beyond the cork oaks and thin pastureland of Leon, the Way of St James climbs over the Sierra de Ancares to reach the wooded slopes of Galicia. It is here that the local smallholders still train their vines in festoons and grow their tiny patches of grain. Along the picturesque and highly indented coast of Galicia are dozens of harbours from which the sardine fishermen put out in their small boats. This northwestern corner of Spain has always been different from the rest of the country, and its inhabitants, speaking a dialect more akin to Portuguese than to Spanish, have always considered themselves to be Galicians first and Spanish second. Though the area was only truly independent between 410 and 585, it seems to have been treated as a separate entity throughout the Middle Ages by the Kings of Leon and Castile. Today the Galicians have their own separatist movement and still feel themselves to be quite distinct.

The greatest treasure of Galicia was, of course, the great pilgrim centre of Santiago de Compostella. Over the tomb of St James has been built one of the greatest churches in Europe. It was begun in 1060 in the Romanesque style and completed less than two centuries later in the same style. The interior is dominated by huge, solid pillars and rounded arches which march in impressive array along the nave and transepts. The 80-foot-tall nave is lined by aisles and a high gallery and runs for an uninterrupted 325 feet towards the altar. Located in the apse is the Capilla Mayor, with its beautiful baroque reliquary, which forms the centre of the entire church. It is here that the mortal remains of St James lie.

To the north lies Corunna, a city which is of almost as much importance to modern trade as Santiago de Compostella was to mediaeval piety. Corunna is one of the most important ports in northern Spain, exporting vast quantities of local produce, importing coal and manufactured goods and engaging in the fishing business in a big way. Four centuries ago, its position on the Atlantic made the fortune of Corunna through trade with the New World, but the loss of the colonies brought an equally important decline which has only been halted in comparatively recent years. Today, a quarter of a million people make their homes here, divided between the Old Town, New Town and modern suburbs. Despite its name, the Old Town does not boast many old buildings, mainly because England's Sir Francis Drake burnt the city down in 1589. The New Town is far more representative, with its miradores – balconies which are glazed in as protection against the ever-present wind.

Two centuries after Sir Francis Drake's escapade another British knight came to Corunna, but this time as a friend. In 1809, the British sent an army to help the Spanish in their revolt against the French. Under Sir John Moore this army executed a series of strategic manoeuvres which held up the French advance for nearly a year. In the process, however, Moore was cut off from his base in Portugal and was forced to retreat to Corunna. Here his army fought a rearguard action against the French before being able to embark on board ship and return to Britain. Sir John Moore was killed in the battle and his tomb remains one of the sights of the city.

Similar in many ways to Corunna is the great port of Cadiz, far to the south. Like Corunna, Cadiz is an ancient city which gained immeasurably from trade with the New World following the discovery of America by Christopher Columbus in 1492. The gold and silver of the Spanish colonies poured into Spain by way of Cadiz and the city became increasingly important for both merchant and naval shipping. In 1587, as the great Armada was being prepared for the invasion of England, Sir Francis Drake visited Cadiz as he was to visit Corunna. Without warning, he appeared off the port with a squadron of ships. Calmly sailing into the harbour, Drake bombarded the city and its shipping. It was during the period of prosperity after Drake's visit that the magnificent New Cathedral was raised beside the harbour. A masterpiece of Classical design and with a magnificent dome, the cathedral took more than a century to build. While the cathedral was being built, Cadiz benefited from British arms in the war with Napoleon, and became the capital of Spain. The decline which set in at Cadiz with the loss of the American colonies was not reversed until early this century, when new port facilities brought a change in fortune. Cadiz makes most of its living by exporting crops and manufactured goods from its hinterland, and from fishing.

This hinterland includes some of the loveliest cities in Spain. About 70 miles up the Guadalquiver River lies Seville, the fourth largest city in the nation. With a long and distinguished history which dates back to pre-Roman times, Seville passed through Visigothic and Muslim hands before falling to the Christians in 1248. Within a few years nearly all the Muslims had left the city, to be replaced by Christians who poured down from the north to take advantage of the new lands and new opportunities. It was not until the 15th century, however, that Seville reached the apogee of its greatness as a cultural centre, a situation which would persist for 300 years.

It was during this period of cultural and economic prosperity that the great buildings of the city were erected. In the 18th century the Palacio de San Telmo was raised on the Avenida de Roma and has long been recognised as one of the finest examples of the distinctive southern-Spanish baroque. Of more orthodox baroque inspiration is the huge Fabrica de Tabacos of 1757. This tobacco factory, now used by the university, is the second-largest building in Spain and presents four beautiful facades to the outside world while keeping 100 courtyards enfolded in its walls. But it is the spectacular 15th-century cathedral which forms the centrepiece of the city, with its many pinnacles and its magnificent west doorway. Within the doorway the sheer elegance of the Gothic interior makes one of the most impressive sights in the city. It is, in fact, the largest Gothic cathedral in Christendom and its clean lines and the well-balanced proportions of its nave make it appear even bigger. Beside the cathedral stands the 300-foot-high Giralda of 1196, once the minaret of a mosque but now converted to a bell tower.

Another Muslim mosque which has been turned to Christian use stands beside the Guadalquiver at Cordova, where a Roman bridge crosses the river. The Cathedral of Cordova began life in 785 as the church of the Emir of Cordova and incorporated 11 aisles. By the close of the 10th century, however, the building had become the principal mosque for western Islam and had grown to six times its original size. The interior of the cathedral is one of the most remarkable places in Spain. Only 35 feet tall, the vast room stretches for more than 400 feet as a forest of pillars. Many of these pillars were taken from ancient buildings and display a variety of colour and design that somehow blends together into an harmonious whole. In the semi-darkness of the shadowy cathedral the red and white arches that top the columns appear like tree branches sprouting from stone trunks. At the heart of this massive mosque the Christians, who captured the city in 1236, built their own church. Set down like a building from another world, the Gothic and baroque edifice of the Christian building jars awkwardly with the delicate Moorish structure.

Many other mediaeval and Renaissance churches and convents testify to the triumph of Christianity over Islam, which could once boast 300 mosques in the city. Yet enough of the Moorish city remains to show what a beautiful place this was in the days when Arabs held sway. Though it is the beautiful churches and Moorish character which draw tourists to Cordova by the thousand, the city is perhaps better known in Spain because of one of its sons. Born in 1936, Manuel Benitez Perez spent his early years in an orphanage and in trouble with the police. After his compulsory service in the army, however, Perez turned to bullfighting. He assumed the name of El Cordobes, 'the man from Cordova', and took the bullfighting world by storm. Though he lacked the elegant air of other bullfighters, El Cordobes wove sharp reflexes, incredible courage and a magical personality into one of the most popular and entertaining performances that has ever graced the ring.

From Cordova the main road runs eastwards along the valley of the Guadalquiver to the small town of Bailen. In the church of Bailen lies the tomb of Castanos y Arragori, the Spanish general who defeated the French here in 1809. From Bailen the road turns north to cross the Sierra Morena at the high pass above Las Correderas. From there it runs northwards across the monotonous high plateaux of New Castile. More than 2,000 feet above sea level, the tablelands have a severe climate with hot, dry summers and bitterly cold winters, and agriculture is generally only possible in irrigated areas. The small clusters of mud-brick houses which lie scattered across the land give way only occasionally to cities.

One such is Toledo, long famous for the quality of its steel. In the earliest days of the Roman Empire in Spain, writers talked about the swords of Toledo, then called Toletum. It seems that from before the time of Christ, the craftsmen of Toledo made steel and experimented with new forms of production. Before the days of mass production, the manufacture of steel was a tricky process, being as much an art as a science, for ore varied in its quality as did the charcoal used to heat it. Only a practised eye could tell when steel should be heated, hammered or cooled. That steel should be of first-rate quality was of vital importance, for a sword blade which cracked or bent in the heat of battle could spell death for its owner. Toledo steel was, therefore, as much a life insurance as a prestige symbol.

Perched on its rocky site above the Tagus, Toledo is often considered the epitome of Spain and has, indeed, been declared a national monument. The steepness of the hill on which the city is built made the city defensible in days gone by, but has always been something of an inconvenience for everyday life. Narrow, winding streets twist beneath the tall buildings to form the haphazard street plan of the city. On the highest point of the hill the Romans built a fortress, and the site is still held by the Alcazar. This great, square building with its four corner towers is the latest of many to occupy the site, previous edifices having been destroyed by the French in 1810 and during the Civil War in 1936. Of all the monasteries and churches which crowd together in the city, the finest and most impressive must be the cathedral, whose tower breaks the skyline in any view of the city. The foundation stone of the cathedral was laid in 1226 and the building was eventually finished in 1493. In most ecclesiastical buildings such a long period of construction resulted in a variety of styles being used, but at Toledo the plan remained unequivocally Gothic. In the 300-foot-tall tower of the cathedral hangs the Campana Gorda, one of the world's most famous bells.

Northeast of Toledo, above the Rio Manzanares, stands Madrid, Spain's largest city. Madrid is a huge city, boasting more than three million inhabitants, and its social life is perhaps the most talked about and admired in Spain. Yet it has not always been so. Seven centuries ago Madrid was as unimportant as dozens of other places in Spain, and that is exactly why it ended up as the capital of the country. When the place known as Majrit was captured by the Christians in 1103 it was conspicuous only by its insignificance. It had been an outlying castle in the defences of Toledo and overlooked no important trade route, was not strongly fortified and had one of the most unpleasant climates in Spain. For the King of Castile and Leon who captured it, Majrit was simply a convenient location in which to hold the Cortes, or Spanish parliament, when he resided in Toledo. However, with the unification of the various Spanish kingdoms in the 16th century the king found that he needed to establish a monarchy which was not identified with any of the preceding dynasties. Castilians would object to a Catalonian king as strongly as the Catalonians would to a king from Leon, but everyone would accept a neutral ruler. So it was that, in 1561, King Philip II brought his court to Madrid, one of the most unimportant, and so least objectionable, towns in his realm.

Madrid did have the advantage of standing more or less

in the geographical centre of the nation and it may have been this fact as much as any other which prompted the king to come here. Amongst the first things that the government did was to establish effective communications with the rest of the country by a series of roads which radiated from the capital. Indeed, the sprawling Plaza Puerta del Sol is still reckoned to be Kilometre 0 in the road system of Spain.

With the business of government in the city, Madrid did not stay small and unimportant for long, and it is the edifices of government which are still the major sights of the city. The palace which Philip II inhabitated during his early years here was based around the castle captured from the Moors centuries earlier, though numerous extensions and modifications had made it more a home than a fortress. In 1734, the entire royal palace burnt to the ground. This gave Philip V the opportunity to build a new palace more befitting the might and prestige of the king of Spain. For 30 years work continued on this imposing building, which still impresses the grand and splendid nature of its royal builder upon the visitor. The severe classical facades of the palace blend well with both the formal gardens which surround it and the statues of the four Spaniards who became Emperors of Rome which grace its courtyard.

While the palace displays the might of kings, the Cathedral to the south glorifies in stone the might of God. Like the palace, the cathedral follows the Classical style, but it remains unfinished, only having been begun in 1883. While this new cathedral awaits completion, a church built in 1626 and dedicated to Saint Isidro, patron of the city, is used as the centre of worship. All around the city are shrines to the greatness of God, for the people of Madrid have always been lavish in their churches, and the many domes and spires are still a feature of a city which has few high-rise buildings to mar the skyline.

Many of the national institutions which have been established in Madrid have somehow felt the urge to commemorate themselves in stone, as the monarchy and church have done. The most impressive of these structures must be the Head Post Office, built in 1911. This extravagant structure of towers, pinnacles and huge doorways is a splendid addition to Madrid, though the locals dubbed it 'Our Lady of Communications', because of its supposed likeness to a cathedral.

Yet all this was not enough for Philip II, one of the greatest of Spanish kings. Perhaps it was too much. After he had spent some time abroad, Philip returned to Spain in 1559 never to leave, and he spent most of his time in Castile. In the hills to the northwest of Madrid Philip built a huge, austere monastery which also served as his palace. Behind the plain, unadorned, granite face of El Escorial, Philip directed the policies of his mighty empire and piously attended church. He sent his legions and ships out to conquer heathens and heretics throughout the world while, in his hilltop retreat, he prayed to God. In the Mediterranean he waged a long and successful war against the Islamic Ottoman Empire, culminating in the bloody naval battle of Lepanto. In Europe he waged a ceaseless campaign against the Protestants, sending armies to the Netherlands and France and launching the massive Armada against England.

He saw himself as carrying out the will of God by imposing the will of the Catholic Church throughout his domains and on those beyond. While embarking on such great works for the strength of the Church, Philip stayed in his monastery and tried to live a life of holiness, in contemplation of the divine. When Philip knew himself to be dying, he lay down in his private cell, which had a tiny aperture which enabled him to witness Mass in the great church he had built in El Escorial, and waited to meet God. Yet in contemplating the holy altar and ceremonies, Philip was turning his back on one of the greatest and most beautiful gifts God could give to him or to any man: Spain.

Facing page: Pyrenean scenery at Planoles, east of La Molina.

Northeastern Spain is distinguished by the magnificent scenery of the Pyrenees (these pages). Facing page and bottom: the Sierra del Boumort region, (bottom left) farm buildings in the village of Alp (overleaf right), near the border with France and (overleaf left) a mountain valley near Oliana.

espite the rapid development of tourist facilities, the natural
Mediterranean beauty of Spain's 'wild coast' – the Costa Brava – is still to be
found at resorts such as Tossa de Mar (facing page), Lloret de Mar (above and
overleaf right) and Calella de Palafrugell (overleaf left).

23

Barcelona, the capital of Catalonia, is Spain's main centre of commerce and industry and also one of the Mediterranean's largest ports. Above: a view northwards across the city and (facing page) the marina and harbour. Overleaf: Barcelona is bounded on the southwest by Montjuich, the site of a great park containing the beautiful Palacio National (right) and fascinating displays from the 1929 International Exhibition, one of which is the Pueblo Español - the Spanish Village (left).

These pages: flower stalls on the main section of Barcelona's Ramblas, a succession of broad avenues, lined with plane trees, linking the Columbus Monument with the Plaza de Cataluña. Overleaf: views northwards over Rambla de Santa Mónica (left), and from Montjuich (right).

Facing page: (top right) the Columbus Monument on the Plaza de la Paz (top left), (bottom left) the Pueblo Seco and (bottom right) sculpture based on regional dance. Below: Barcelona Cathedral, (bottom) a tower in the Pueblo Español, and (right) La Sagrada Familia.

Previous pages: morning mist (left) and golden sun (right) over the Montserrat massif, northwest of Barcelona. These pages: views of the island of Mallorca, including (below) farmland near Santañi and (bottom) irrigation near Horta de Sa Pobla, (right) Puerto de Sóller, (bottom right) Santa Maria, and (facing page) Puerto de Pollensa.

The attractive town of Puerto de Pollensa (previous pages) is one of the major resorts in Mallorca, the largest of the Balearic Islands. With their mild climate and beautiful landscapes of pine forests and perfect beaches, the Balearics, which also comprise Menorca and Ibiza, are popular with tourists for most of the year. Facing page: (top left) Cala Galdana, (bottom left) the harbour of Fornells, and (bottom right) the maritime area of Mahon, all in Menorca. Top right: the coast of Portinatx, Ibiza, and (above) sunrise over the landscape near Ibiza town.

Dominating the harbour of Palma, capital of Mallorca and of the whole archipelago, is a great Gothic cathedral (top left), built between 1230 and 1600. Above: the interior of Ibiza's cathedral, which tops the hill upon which the Carthaginians built Ibiza town (remaining pictures) in 654 BC.

One of the main resorts on the Costa del Azahar is Peñiscola (these pages), perched on a rocky, fortified peninsula jutting into the Mediterranean. This picturesque town is dominated by a fine medieval castle, next to which is the pretty Church of the Virgen de la Ermitana (above and top right).

estiges of the small fishing village that Benidorm (these and previous pages) nce was are still to be found in this now famous tourist resort. Beyond the oncrete jungle of hotels, the old town still clusters around a domed church n a rocky promontory, overlooking a sea still trawled by native fishermen.

Overleaf: northeast of Benidorm, on the cliff-fringed Costa Blanca, or 'white coast', and beyond the attractive resort of Altea (right), is the charming fishing town of Calpe with its magnificent geological formation, the Peñon de Ifach (left), rising like a lesser Rock of Gibraltar over the Mediterranean.

These pages: local crafts and produce at Purullena in the Guadix area, famous for its extraordinary cave dwellings. Overleaf: north of the town of Almeria is the landscape (right) of barren mountains and desert used in the filming of *Lawrence of Arabia,* and the set at Little Hollywood (left) where westerns such as *A Fistful of Dollars* were shot.

Perched high on a hill overlooking the city of Granada (bottom) is one of Europe's most famous and enchanting monuments, the Alhambra (remaining pictures). Overleaf: this exquisite Moorish complex is enhanced by the gardens of the Generalife (left) and of the Portal (right).

Facing page: Granada seen from the Alhambra (this page), which comprises three groups of buildings; the original 11th-century fortress called the Alcazaba, the 14th-century Royal Palace, with its tranquil Court of Myrtles (right), and the Generalife Palace, with its exquisite gardens (above).

It is widely accepted that Moorish art reached its zenith in the Royal Palace of the Alhambra, which was largely the creation of the 14th-century kings Yusuf I and Mohammed V. The grace and balance of its architecture is illustrated by the elegant Ladies' Tower (previous pages left), which overlooks the Portal Gardens eulogised by Arab poets of old, and in the fantastic Court of Lions (previous pages right and above), with its arcade supported by a forest of slender columns. The Palace's fantastically ornate interior decor (top) has become world famous, leading to a style known as 'Alhambra'. Facing page left: the Patio of the Stream in the gardens of the Generalife (remaining pictures), which is thought to mean 'the sublime orchard'.

ne of the oldest parts of Granada is the eastern suburb of Sacromonte,
ituated on Mount Valparaiso. In this fascinating village of gipsy cave
wellings stands an elegant Benedictine abbey (these pages), with a fine
med chapel. Overleaf: the northern Sierra Nevada, which provides

Granada with a startling backdrop. Only a couple of hours drive from the
sweltering sands of the Costa del Sol, these majestic snowy mountains offer
good skiing during most of the year.

Top: sunset-coloured rocks in the Sierra Nevada (overleaf), where snow-capped El Veleta (top right), Spain's second highest mountain, looms over green fields. Right: a mule-drawn plough in the nearby Monachil area, and (above and facing page) olive groves near Moclin, northeast of Granada.

Right: white houses in the attractive town of Salobreña, on the coast near Motril, and (below, bottom and bottom right) views from the Pinos Genil area, just east of Granada, of the Sierra Nevada (facing page), above which magnificent sunsets are frequent (overleaf).

hese pages and overleaf: views of the southern slopes of the Sierra Nevada
om Capileira, which is one of the 'high villages' in this region of fertile
lleys known as the Alpujarras. With their white, flat-roofed box houses
acing page), the villages have changed little architecturally since they were
tablished by the Berbers in the 13th century.

81

These pages: country life in the province of Granada, where the pace is slow.
Above and facing page top left: chrysanthemum cultivation and (facing page
bottom right) goats being herded, near Motril, and (facing page top right) a
lady crocheting in a village near Orgiva, in the Alpujarras.

Torremolinos (this page), the little village that grew up in the 1800s around the towers and mills that its name refers to, is now one of the Costa del Sol's busiest resorts, providing a plethora of bars, restaurants and hotels. Facing page: flowers decorating houses in the resort of Salobreña (overleaf), near Motril.

Above: the rugged coast of Almuñecar, on the Costa del Sol, and (facing page)
evening light on nearby Salobreña, the focal point of which is a ruined
Moorish castle, circumvallated by the remains of a medieval wall.
Glamorous Malaga (overleaf), is the major resort of this region, and one of
the oldest ports in the Mediterranean.

Boasting a magnificent location in the mountainous countryside (below) east of Antequera is the little town of Archidona (these pages), where a gleaming white monastery (bottom left) perches on a hill with the ruins of a medieval castle (bottom).

The ruins of a Moorish castle (facing page top right) loom over Antequera
(these pages), a beautiful town situated in the verdant valley of the
Guadalhorce River, at the foot of the Sierra del Torcal.

Top right: a ruined castle near Almargen, west of Antequera, and (above) farmland further west, near Olvera (facing page), a striking town with a fine cathedral and the keep and walls of a old castle. Southwest of Olvera, in the Sierra Margarita (top), is Zahara (right), once a border stronghold of the province of Malaga.

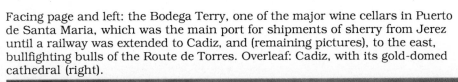

Facing page and left: the Bodega Terry, one of the major wine cellars in Puerto de Santa Maria, which was the main port for shipments of sherry from Jerez until a railway was extended to Cadiz, and (remaining pictures), to the east, bullfighting bulls of the Route de Torres. Overleaf: Cadiz, with its gold-domed cathedral (right).

These pages: Andalusia's magnificent capital city, Seville, situated on the banks of the Guadalquivir River (above). Facing page: the Palacio Español on the Plaza de España, (top left) the Santa Cruz quarter, (top) the lush Plaza de America, and (left) the 305-foot-high Giralda tower, overlooking the Banderas Patio.

Previous pages: Seville is noted for its parks, one of the finest being the Parque de Maria Luisa, which contains buildings from the 1929 Spanish-American exhibition, including the semicircular Palacio Español in the Plaza de España (left) and the Mudejar Pavilion (right) in the Plaza de America. East of Seville along the Guadalquivir River is Cordoba, a fascinating city of Moorish character, with a fine 14th-century castle (facing page bottom right) and, most importantly, the magnificent cathedral (remaining pictures) that was once the principal mosque of the western Islamic world. Overleaf: (left) Cordoba's Roman Bridge, which was rebuilt by the Arabs, and (right) a market in the Plaza de la Corredera.

One of the most picturesque old towns in central Spain is Cuenca (these pages) in New Castile. Situated above the deep valleys of the Jucar and Huecar rivers, it is noted for its 'hanging houses' (below), called Casas Colgadas, which date from the 14th century.

On a plateau in New Castile, at the geographical centre of the Iberian Peninsula, is Madrid, made the capital of Spain in 1606 by King Philip III. Some of Europe's finest classical architecture is to be found here, such as the Puerta de Alcala (facing page), a great triumphal arch commissioned by Charles III and built in 1778, and the superb Royal Palace (below), which was built for Philip V between 1738 and 1764 on the site of the former Alcazar, or castle. Opposite the palace and the Plaza de la Armeria (far right) is the Plaza de Oriente, which contains a fine equestrian statue of Philip IV (right) and 44 statues (bottom right) of Spanish kings and queens. Overleaf: (right) the fountain of the goddess Cybele, with her lion-drawn carriage, on the Plaza de la Cibeles, backed by Madrid's General Post Office, which was built 1904-18. Left: a panorama of Toledo, with its Gothic cathedral and great, square fortress dominating the horizon.

The largest and loveliest of Madrid's parks is the Parque de Retiro (these pages), which was originally the garden of a summer palace built by Philip II. The palace was burnt down in 1734 and the focal point of the park is now a large artificial lake (left and bottom left). Overlooking this is the magnificent Monument to Alfonso XII (facing page), surrounded by a gracious colonnade.

Perched on a 330-foot-high hill on the northern slopes of the Sierra de Guadarrama is the magical city of Segovia (these pages), famed for its Roman aqueduct (left) and beautiful, turreted Alcazar (top and overleaf left). Also of note is the late Gothic cathedral (facing page and overleaf right), which is known as the 'Lady of Spanish cathedrals'.

Bottom right: the new cathedral, with adjoining old cathedral, in the ancient university town of Salamanca, and (below) the harbour of one of northern Spain's major ports, Santander, to the east of which is the rocky coastline (bottom) and little town of Castro Urdiales (facing page), dominated by its great, Gothic church (right).

Tenerife, the largest of the Canary Islands (these pages), offers a great variety of scenery, including Mount Teide (top left), Spain's highest peak, the Beach of the Americas (left), the bays and pools of Garachico (top) and the harbour of Los Christianos (above). Facing page: the salt-pans of Janubio and (overleaf) camels in the volcanic landscape of Timanfaya, in Lanzarote.